NIST Cybersecurity Framework

A pocket guide

NIST Cybersecurity Framework

A pocket guide

Alan Calder

IT Governance Publishing

Every possible effort has been made to ensure that the information contained in this book is accurate at the time of going to press, and the publisher and the author cannot accept responsibility for any errors or omissions, however caused. Any opinions expressed in this book are those of the author, not the publisher. Websites identified are for reference only, not endorsement, and any website visits are at the reader's own risk. No responsibility for loss or damage occasioned to any person acting, or refraining from action, as a result of the material in this publication can be accepted by the publisher or the author.

Apart from any fair dealing for the purposes of research or private study, or criticism or review, as permitted under the Copyright, Designs and Patents Act 1988, this publication may only be reproduced, stored or transmitted, in any form, or by any means, with the prior permission in writing of the publisher or, in the case of reprographic reproduction, in accordance with the terms of licences issued by the Copyright Licensing Agency. Enquiries concerning reproduction outside those terms should be sent to the publisher at the following address:

IT Governance Publishing Ltd
Unit 3, Clive Court
Bartholomew's Walk
Cambridgeshire Business Park
Ely, Cambridgeshire
CB7 4EA
United Kingdom

www.itgovernancepublishing.co.uk

© Alan Calder 2018

The author has asserted the rights of the author under the Copyright, Designs and Patents Act, 1988, to be identified as the author of this work.

First published in the United Kingdom in 2018 by IT Governance Publishing.
ISBN 978-1-78778-040-8

ABOUT THE AUTHOR

Alan Calder is the founder and executive chairman of IT Governance USA Inc (*www.itgovernanceusa.com*), an information, advice, and consultancy firm that helps company boards tackle IT governance, risk management, compliance, and information security issues. Alan is an acknowledged international cybersecurity guru, and a leading author on information security and IT governance issues. He has many years of senior management experience in the private and public sectors.

vi

CONTENTS

INTRODUCTION

Cybersecurity is becoming an ever more important facet of business, especially for organizations that operate infrastructure and essential services. There are 16 critical infrastructure sectors in the U.S. which provide physical and digital services that the national and economic security of the nation depends on.[1] If any harm were to come to them, revenue could suffer, costs would be driven up, and it could even place public safety and health at risk, in addition to the U.S. security and economy.

The U.S. Department of Homeland Security (DHS) lists the following critical infrastructure sectors:

- Chemical
- Commercial facilities
- Communications
- Critical manufacturing
- Dams
- Defense industrial base
- Emergency services
- Energy
- Financial services
- Food and agriculture
- Government facilities
- Health care and public health
- Information technology (IT)
- Nuclear reactors, materials, and waste
- Transportation systems
- Water and wastewater systems

---

[1] DHS, "Critical Infrastructure Sectors", July 2017, *www.dhs.gov/critical-infrastructure-sectors*.

The growing digital ecosystem

These sectors increasingly depend on IT and industrial control systems (ICS). ICS are now an integral part of a number of industries, and are implemented where human control would either be inadequate or incapable. This includes processes like power plant switches, light controls and warning signs in traffic systems, air traffic control, and the handling of materials. ICS are increasingly integrating with IT networks, not to mention that many other functions within critical infrastructure are at least partly reliant on IT.

The reliability of the U.S. critical infrastructure sectors is vital to maintaining the American way of life. These IT and ICS dependencies, however, provide an ever-growing attack surface for cyber criminals, which threatens that reliability. This is in addition to the rising number of cyber attacks – most notably conducted by Russia, China, North Korea, and Iran.[2]

Such attacks attempt to exploit vulnerabilities at any point in the organization, whether through social engineering, viruses and malware, network- and application-layer attacks, or any of the myriad of other methods. They typically target either software and networks that drive critical business functions and/or control systems that operate physical processes. Examples of each are respectively client databases and railroad switches. The substantial damages, resulting from fines, lawsuits, lost turnover, and damaged intellectual property, have both financial and reputational impacts.

Federal responses

In response to the rising number of threats, President Obama issued Executive Order 13636 (EO) titled "Improving Critical Infrastructure Cybersecurity" in February 2013. The EO called for a voluntary, risk-based cybersecurity framework to be

---

[2] DSB, "Task Force on Cyber Deterrence", February 2017, *www.acq.osd.mil/dsb/reports/2010s/DSB-CyberDeterrenceReport_02-28-17_Final.pdf*.

developed, outlining best practice for critical infrastructure sectors to manage their cybersecurity risks effectively. The result of this initiative was Version 1.0 of the "Framework for Improving Critical Infrastructure Cybersecurity" (CSF), which was developed in collaboration with industry, and published by the National Institute of Standards and Technology (NIST) in February 2014.

This first CSF was superseded by Version 1.1 in April 2018,[3] which was formalized and partly evolved on the basis of the Cybersecurity Enhancement Act of 2014 (CEA), passed in December 2014, calling for a "prioritized, flexible, repeatable, performance-based, and cost-effective approach, including information security measures and controls that may be voluntarily adopted by owners and operators of critical infrastructure to help them identify, assess, and manage cyber risks". This pocket guide will focus on the NIST CSF and discuss it in more detail.

Another federal response to the rising number of threats was the President's National Infrastructure Advisory Council (NIAC) report dating back to August 2017.[4] This report made 11 recommendations regarding the cybersecurity of critical infrastructure. While many of them require a certain degree of collaboration within each sector, there are some recommendations that individual organizations could completely or mostly implement themselves. These are:

- Establishing separate, secure communications networks
- Identifying and implementing scanning tools and assessment practices

---

[3] See the appendix of this pocket guide for an overview of the main changes from Version 1.0 to 1.1.

[4] NIAC, "Securing Cyber Assets – Addressing Urgent Cyber Threats to Critical Infrastructure", August 2017, *www.dhs.gov/sites/default/files/publications/niac-securing-cyber-assets-final-report-508.pdf*.

- Establishing policies to quickly declassify cyber threat information
- Optimizing the cybersecurity governance approach

Past cyber incidents

Unsurprisingly, as the number of cyber attacks grows, so does the number that are successful. In March 2018, the FBI and DHS issued an alert that there had been a spike in cyber criminal activity since at least March 2016.[5] This alert was specifically aimed at the Russian government targeting critical infrastructure, particularly the energy sector.

Dragonfly, a well-known hacking group active since 2011, appears to be heavily involved with the cyber crime spike. The group primarily targets European and North American critical infrastructure operators, with a focus on those in the energy sector. Dragonfly has demonstrated technical capability and appears to work in phases, with each step becoming more menacing. So far, it has used a wide range of techniques that include intelligence gathering, sabotage, spear phishing, Trojanized software, and watering hole websites.[6]

A more recent example was the 2017 Equifax data breach, where criminal hackers compromised the consumer data of at least 147.9 million people around the world by exploiting the organization's poor cybersecurity practices. So far, the breach has cost Equifax more than $242 million,[7] and led to a great deal

---

[5] US-CERT, "Alert (TA18-074A) – Russian Government Cyber Activity Targeting Energy and Other Critical Infrastructure Sectors", March 2018, *www.us-cert.gov/ncas/alerts/TA18-074A*.

[6] Security Response Attack Investigation Team, "Dragonfly: Western energy sector targeted by sophisticated attack group", *Symantec*, October 2017, *www.symantec.com/blogs/threat-intelligence/dragonfly-energy-sector-cyber-attacks*.

[7] Doug Olenick, "Equifax data breach cost hits £175 million - £91 million insured", *SC Media*, April 2018,

of criticism for both failing to patch a known vulnerability and taking over a month to publicly announce the breach.[8]

Attacks do not only target networks and IT systems in pursuit of data, however – they can have immediately tangible effects in the physical world. The infamous Stuxnet computer worm targeted an Iranian nuclear plant in 2010, causing significant physical damage. Stuxnet attacked the programmable logic controllers that managed the centrifuges, changing spinning speeds, which caused the centrifuges to disintegrate, and significantly affected Iran's nuclear program. Stuxnet was considered the world's first digital weapon, despite originating from a humble USB stick.[9] It has since been used as the basis for new worms: Duqu, Flame, and Gauss.[10]

In 2014, the German Federal Office for Information Security reported an incident in which cyber attackers interfered with ICS, which caused physical damage to a German steel plant. In this case, the attacker used spear phishing and sophisticated social engineering techniques. These intrusions led to the malfunctioning of various key ICS components, eventually causing a blast furnace to shut down, resulting in 'massive' (though unspecified) damage.[11]

---

www.scmagazineuk.com/equifax-data-breach-cost-hits-175-million-- 91-million-insured/article/761618/.
[8] Senator Elizabeth Warren, "Bad Credit: Uncovering Equifax's Failure to Protect Americans' Personal Information", February 2018, *www.documentcloud.org/documents/4368610-Equifax-Report- Interactive-FINAL.html.*
[9] David Kushner, "The Real Story of Stuxnet", *IEEE Spectrum,* February 2013, *https://spectrum.ieee.org/telecom/security/the-real- story-of-stuxnet.*
[10] Boldizsár Bencsáth, Gábor Pék, Levente Buttyán, and Márk Félegyházi, "The Cousins of Stuxnet: Duqu, Flame, and Gauss", *Future Internet,* November 2012, *www.mdpi.com/1999- 5903/4/4/971/pdf.*
[11] BSI, "Bericht zur Lage der IT-Sicherheit in Deutschland 2014", December 2014,

Another notable incident occurred in 2015, when Ukraine fell victim to the first confirmed attack to target a power grid.[12] A well-organized group of criminal hackers is believed to have used BlackEnergy malware, delivered via spear phishing emails, to gain access to critical devices at three regional power distribution companies. This enabled the intruders to overwrite those devices, cutting power to approximately 225,000 Ukrainian customers for up to six hours.

On the face of it, the physical damage as a result of interfering with ICS did not seem particularly large. However, it took many months for the control center to become fully operational again, which was partly due to different malware, KillDisk, which "erases selected files on target systems and corrupts the master boot record, rendering systems inoperable".[13] A further three Ukrainian companies, in different critical infrastructure sectors, reported that they had been infected by similar malware, though they did not experience operational impacts.

The NIST Cybersecurity Framework

The NIST Framework is designed to protect organizations from attacks like these. Although it was originally developed to help U.S. organizations involved in infrastructure systematically organize their cybersecurity activities and ensure they remain up to date, NIST reported that the Framework "has since proven flexible enough to be adopted voluntarily by large and small

---

www.bsi.bund.de/SharedDocs/Downloads/DE/BSI/Publikationen/Lage berichte/Lagebericht2014.html.

[12] Kim Zetter, "Inside the Cunning, Unprecedented Hack of Ukraine's Power Grid", *Wired*, March 2016, www.wired.com/2016/03/inside-cunning-unprecedented-hack-ukraines-power-grid/.

[13] ICS-CERT, "Alert (IR-ALERT-H-16-056-01) – Cyber-Attack Against Ukrainian Critical Infrastructure", February 2016, https://ics-cert.us-cert.gov/alerts/IR-ALERT-H-16-056-01.

companies and organizations across all industry sectors, as well as by federal, state and local governments".[14]

The Framework is also not limited to bodies in the U.S.: "Corporations, organizations and countries around the world, including Italy, Israel and Uruguay, have adopted the framework, or their own adaptation of it".[15] The increasing use is supported by several high-profile industry surveys. Furthermore, President Trump released Executive Order 13800 in May 2017, titled "Strengthening the Cybersecurity of Federal Networks and Critical Infrastructure", which directs federal agencies to the NIST Cybersecurity Framework. Agency heads are mandated to use the Framework to manage their cybersecurity risk, and to provide a risk management report to the Secretary of Homeland Security and the Director of the Office of Management and Budget (OMB).

In its updated version, the Framework has been further refined and clarified, but contains no fundamental changes, making it easily implementable by both existing and new users. The CSF is still strongly focused on making sure that any cybersecurity measures taken are appropriate for the level of risk involved – in other words, ensuring that implemented measures are cost-effective.

---

[14] NIST, "NIST Releases Version 1.1 of its Popular Cybersecurity Framework", April 2018, *www.nist.gov/news-events/news/2018/04/nist-releases-version-11-its-popular-cybersecurity-framework*.
[15] Ibid.

CHAPTER 1: AIMS OF THE FRAMEWORK

In its own words, NIST states in Section 2.0 of the Framework:

> The Framework provides a common language for understanding, managing, and expressing cybersecurity risk both to internal and external stakeholders. It can be used to help identify and prioritize actions for reducing cybersecurity risk, and it is a tool for aligning policy, business, and technological approaches to managing that risk. It can be used to manage cybersecurity risk across entire organizations or it can be focused on the delivery of critical services within an organization. Different types of entities – including sector coordinating structures, associations, and organizations – can use the Framework for different purposes […].

In short, the CSF is a voluntary framework, providing guidance for organizations to help manage their cybersecurity risks. This guidance is based on existing best-practice standards and guidelines, and provides a way of making other frameworks and control sets align with each organization's unique cybersecurity needs.

In order to understand how to secure your information, you first need to know what 'security' really entails. From a crude perspective, you might say that you simply want to stop criminals accessing your information. This is a laudable goal, but really only a fraction of what security is about. Information needs to be protected on three fronts:

- **Confidentiality**
  Information should only be accessible to those who need access to it.

- **Integrity**
  Information should be protected from unauthorized modification, destruction, and loss.

- **Availability**
  The information should be accessible to authorized persons as and when necessary.

Information is, after all, only useful if you know it is correct and you are able to access it. Protecting confidentiality alone does not constitute security. This is especially true for critical infrastructure, when inaccurate or inaccessible data can impact the real world, and may even threaten lives.

While the CSF is applicable to any organization in any part of the world, which is particularly true of Version 1.1, its primary audience is organizations heavily involved in critical infrastructure. Organizations intending to get into the critical infrastructure supply chain may also want to take note of this framework.

The Framework specifies in its executive summary that it is "a living document and will continue to be updated and improved as industry provides feedback on implementation". As past experiences are taken note of, and the lessons learned from them are integrated into newer versions, the CSF will be continually improved and kept up to date with ever-evolving "threats, risks, and solutions".

Relevant factors and variables

The CSF provides general guidance, with more specific guidance on implementing cybersecurity controls provided by existing sources. The specifics for an organization implementing cybersecurity defenses and procedures will naturally vary, depending on the organization's size, sector, business needs, and objectives. Such business objectives might be to meet the minimum standards for a series of contract bids, which are likely to be made very clear by the contracting organizations, or to reach a defined level of maturity. The objectives could also be inspired by past disruptions that had an impact on productivity, in which case it is likely that there are clear metrics to aim for. The previously mentioned reliance on IT and ICS is another significant variable.

In addition to these, each organization will need to identify the types of threats and typical vulnerabilities it faces, besides determining its risk appetite. An organization that relies on ancient software and systems, for instance, will have very different needs than an organization that operates largely in the Cloud. Furthermore, the potential harm from any given incident could be considered negligible, or perhaps tolerable if the organization is pursuing specific opportunities.

Implementation benefits

The CSF can be used to establish an entirely new cybersecurity program, improve an existing one, or simply provide an opportunity to review the organization's cybersecurity practices. By implementing the Framework in accordance with their own specific circumstances, organizations are able to manage their cybersecurity risks in the most cost-effective way possible, maximizing the return on investment in the organization's security. Furthermore, as the CSF incorporates response and recovery, the organization benefits from being able to quickly return to business as usual, while minimizing the risk of an incident in the first place.

It also provides a 'common language', optimizing communication both within the organization and with external partners. Using such a common language naturally helps limit confusion as to what is meant in contracts and other second- or third-party agreements. In addition, contract opportunities improve by meeting higher minimum standards. Likewise, opportunities to operate in other jurisdictions increase, as good practice tends to align with legal requirements.

Furthermore, implementing a framework of best practice – particularly a framework that combines various sources of guidance, in addition to being a framework for cybersecurity – provides valuable experience in meeting compliance requirements that the organization can use to meet other, and perhaps newer, standards and obligations, whether these are legal, contractual, or imposed by stakeholders.

As the CSF draws upon various best-practice guidelines, your organization may already have a good chunk of NIST's recommended controls in place. However, your organization may also want to secure itself and have a structure in place to meet any later requirements. Such an approach would strengthen your existing measures, recommend guidance for areas of weakness, and let you implement any additional measures that may be necessary. Furthermore, by making sure that you identify the organization's current practices first, you avoid unnecessary, duplicated work.

It is also an excellent way for communicating cybersecurity requirements to stakeholders, ensuring they are made aware of any risks to the organization. This clarity improves the likelihood that investments necessary to reduce or mitigate those risks will be provided, increases awareness throughout the organization, and gains customers' trust by letting them know that you are protecting their data, in addition to their access to infrastructure and essential services.

Being able to effectively communicate with external partners will also help you to keep up to date with constantly evolving cybersecurity threats and technologies – particularly those that are relevant to your industry or sector. While being aware of what is going on in your industry is always sensible, it also gives your organization the opportunity to improve existing defenses, or implement new ones, based on any information you may receive from partners.

Structure

The Framework has a relatively simple structure with three key components:

- **Core**
  The core comprises the organization's cybersecurity activities and controls.
- **Profiles**
  The profiles map the organization's cybersecurity development.

- **Implementation tiers**
  The tiers describe the level of sophistication of the organization's cybersecurity.

The following chapters will explain each component in more detail.

CHAPTER 2: FRAMEWORK CORE

The Framework core ('core') is, in essence, the actual cybersecurity functions that protect your organization. It takes a structured approach to managing cybersecurity risk, and outlines the key outcomes of implementing the Framework. The core has four elements:

- Functions
- Categories
- Subcategories
- Informative references

Figure 1 illustrates the core structure.

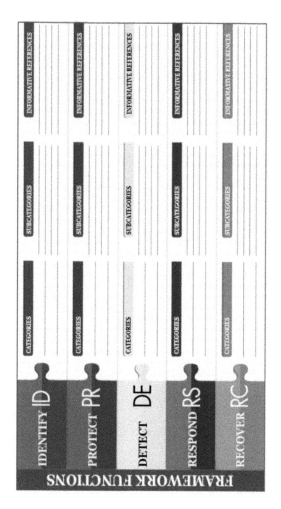

Figure 1: Framework core structure (Source: NIST Cybersecurity Framework, Section 2.1)

Functions

The core recognises five functions that outline how to organize cybersecurity activities:

1. **Identify** potential cybersecurity risks to your information assets
2. **Protect** yourself against these risks by developing and implementing safeguards
3. **Detect** any irregular activity to determine if breaches have occurred
4. **Respond** to any detected breaches to contain their impact
5. **Recover** from these breaches by restoring any undermined assets

This approach to cybersecurity is broader than some other common definitions, and includes processes that might ordinarily be considered part of a larger set of practices generally referred to as 'cyber resilience'. Cyber resilience combines cybersecurity or information security with business continuity, ensuring the organization not only minimizes the likelihood and impact of cyber attacks and other incidents but also improves how it responds to and ultimately recovers from those incidents.

Assuming that a breach *will* happen at some point is good practice in any case, considering that major breaches can even happen to relatively secure organizations – consider Ukraine's power outages in 2015, whose ICS are significantly more secure than some in the U.S.[16] Ultimately, given enough opportunities and resources, cyber criminals can compromise any organization, regardless of size or sector. It also does not help that an organization has to patch *all* of its vulnerabilities and defend against *all* types of attacks, when cyber criminals need to find just *one* weakness to infiltrate and potentially cause damage. Such threats are significant not just because they are difficult to stop, but also because they are increasingly within reach of even common criminals because the tools they use can be replicated and reused as readily as any other information.

---

[16] "Inside the Cunning, Unprecedented Hack of Ukraine's Power Grid".

The CSF itself does not propose alternative functions for different sectors, or suggest that organizations should develop their own functions. However, some industry bodies, such as the Financial Services Sector Coordinating Council (FSSCC), have proposed slight changes relevant for their sectors. The FSSCC has drawn particular attention to two additional functions that are "of priority to the [financial services sector]": governance, which the default Framework includes as an identify category, and supply chain/dependency management.[17] In doing so, it hopes to encourage relevant organizations to look at these additions with a greater degree of granularity than their previous subdivision statuses would suggest.

Organizations are also free to make comparable adjustments if they find it necessary or valuable – a point that is emphatically maintained from Version 1.0. Such adjustments might be in response to a wider movement in the sector, contractual obligations, or any of the other previously mentioned factors that may vary across sectors or organizations.

Identify

While the identify function covers asset management, a natural place to start, it also goes further to include the identification of the business environment, governance, and a risk management strategy. The latter also includes conducting a risk assessment.

As such, the three key things covered within this function are:

1. Determining the business environment, which includes identifying:
   o The organization's role in its sector, and critical infrastructure as a whole
   o Organizational objectives and requirements
   o The organization's role in the supply chain

---

[17] FSSCC, 'Financial Services Sector Specific Cybersecurity "Profile" – NIST Cybersecurity Workshop', May 2017, *www.nist.gov/sites/default/files/documents/2017/05/18/financial_servic es_csf.pdf*.

2. Making cybersecurity and the implementation project topics the board or senior management engages with and oversees, and in doing so prove that the organization takes cybersecurity seriously. Moreover, this ensures that the project is in line with organizational strategies and other projects, and ensures adequate resources will be made available.

3. After completing these two points, you can feed them into the risk management process – an essential step in the success of any cybersecurity project. As we will discuss later, risk management must be conducted with a thorough understanding of the organization's context, strategies, and objectives.

Protect, detect, and respond

It is often asserted that there are three types of cybersecurity control, which align with the protect, detect, and respond functions:

- Preventive
- Detective
- Reactive

Preventive controls can be associated with the protect function. These controls are designed to either stop certain attacks from happening at all, or to reduce their likelihood. Such controls typically include firewalls and malware protection.

The controls that are generally associated with the detect function – those that look for evidence of events and incidents – are designed to assist that process. Whenever anomalous activity on the network is spotted, appropriate personnel and/or systems should be alerted. Two common ways of detecting and countering any breaches are intrusion detection systems (IDSs) and event monitoring.

An IDS automatically monitors access to your organization's networks, and will alert you to any potentially malicious activities or policy violations. Event monitoring, on the other hand, is a way of detecting any breaches or suspicious activity. It includes log collection, management, and analysis. This makes it possible to manually evaluate information about the origin of an incident, identify trends, and make decisions to avoid potential problems.

Finally, reactive controls are designed to support the response and recovery functions. They include processes that assist the quarantine process when an attacker has been discovered, isolating the breached network segment, and preventing the attacker from continuing or exfiltrating data. Reactive and detective controls are designed to reduce the impact of a breach, rather than prevent one from happening at all.

Some controls can fit into multiple categories. For instance, a firewall is primarily preventive, but could also be a detective control. CCTV cameras are primarily detective, but can also act preventively in the sense that they may scare off potential intruders. On top of that, they can help track down an intruder in the aftermath of an intrusion, allowing stolen materials to be recovered, thus acting reactively too.

Recover

Business continuity and continual improvement play large roles in the recover function. After having responded to an incident and stabilized the situation, it is time to fully recover. This implies actually returning to the status quo, rather than just running on minimally acceptable functionality, in addition to taking action to prevent the incident from recurring. This recovery can happen wholesale or in stages.

Each organization will take a different path to full recovery in line with the nature and size of the incident, as well as the organization's specific circumstances, but every organization should have a recovery plan in place. You may wish to take the approach that securing essential services and resilient suppliers will be critical to the recovery process, which is something you can prepare for in advance, long before an incident actually occurs.

Appendix A of the CSF also lists as subcategories of the improvements category (recover function) "Recovery plans incorporate lessons learned" and "Recovery strategies are updated". These practices help to improve an organization's resilience to attacks as well as improving the recovering processes themselves – and if you must suffer a cyber attack or other disruption, you might as well get something positive out of it.

Categories

The CSF supplies a common set of categories across all critical infrastructure sectors in Appendix A. Categories describe general cybersecurity activities, and Appendix A clarifies their purpose in relation to cybersecurity by assigning each of them an objective. See Table 1 for examples.

Table 1: Category examples, aligned to their relevant functions

Function	Category
Identify	Risk assessment
Protect	Identity management and access control
Detect	Security continuous monitoring
Respond	Analysis
Recover	Recovery planning

However, these may differ per organization, and as pointed out in Appendix A, "While the Framework is not exhaustive, it is extensible" – the categories provided are designed to be a starting point only. "Activities can be selected from the Framework Core during the Profile creation process and additional Categories, Subcategories, and Informative References may be added to the Profile". Ultimately, each organization is expected to determine the categories that are appropriate to managing its unique cybersecurity risks effectively.

Subcategories

Subcategories are subdivisions of categories, describing specific results of the activities – which might be technical and/or organizational – required to fulfill each category. In other words, subcategories are controls to ensure each category has been adequately implemented.

Once again, Appendix A of the CSF supplies a common set of subcategories that might apply across all critical infrastructure sectors. Examples of such subcategories, aligned to their relevant categories and functions, are presented in Table 2.

Table 2: Examples of subcategories, aligned to their relevant categories and functions

Function	Category	Subcategory
Identify	Risk assessment	Threats, both internal and external, are identified and documented
Protect	Identity management and access control	Remote access is managed
Detect	Security continuous monitoring	Vulnerability scans are performed
Respond	Analysis	Forensics are performed
Recover	Recovery planning	Recovery plan is executed during or after a cybersecurity incident

Again, these are likely to vary across organizations, as they are expected to determine which subcategories would most effectively manage specifically their risks.

Informative references

Informative references, in turn, are references for subcategories that specify sources of best practice from a range of publications, including standards and guidelines. These describe methods or points of consideration to help achieve the outcomes of each subcategory (or control).

The CSF refers to a relatively small number of sources, which are listed and described below:

- ISO/IEC 27001:2013 (ISO 27001)
- COBIT® 5 (COBIT)
- NIST Special Publication 800-53 Revision 4 (NIST SP 800-53)
- ISA 62443-2-1:2009 4.2.3 and ISA 62443-3-3:2013 (ISA 62443)
- Center for Internet Security (CIS) Critical Security Controls for Effective Cyber Defense (CSC)

ISO 27001

ISO 27001 is the international standard for a best-practice information security management system (ISMS). An ISMS is a systematic approach to making sure confidential or sensitive information remains secure, and its controls and processes generally fall into the identify, protect, and detect functions.

The Standard describes a management system, rather than mandating specific technologies or restricting itself to IT departments, meaning that organizations of any size or sector can implement it. ISO 27001 is also very compatible with other frameworks and standards.

The Standard has a table of "Reference control objectives and controls" in Annex A, which is what the core's informative references relate to. This reference control set is supported by comprehensive implementation guidance in ISO/IEC 27002:2013 (ISO 27002). This expanded guidance builds on a structured approach described in ISO 27001 that helps organizations select controls to mitigate risks.

COBIT

COBIT is a framework, developed by ISACA®, intended to help organizations govern and manage enterprise IT effectively. It is aligned with several other best-practice standards and frameworks, including ISO 27001 and ITIL®. Its most recent version, COBIT 5, was released in 2012.

COBIT is based on five principles:

1. Meeting stakeholder needs
2. Covering the enterprise end to end
3. Applying a single integrated framework
4. Enabling a holistic approach
5. Separating governance from management

COBIT 5 is fundamentally a set of controls that can be applied within a framework to ensure that IT is governed in line with larger business strategies, and that the organization's strategic goals then filter down to user level.

NIST SP 800-53

NIST SP 800-53 is a large set of security and privacy controls intended for federal information systems and organizations, which also features a process for selecting controls. The controls are also meant to be customizable, and "implemented as part of an organization-wide process that manages information security and privacy risk".[18]

---

[18] NIST, "Security and Privacy Controls for Federal Information Systems and Organizations", January 2015, https://csrc.nist.gov/publications/detail/sp/800-53/rev-4/final.

There are 17 categories of controls, which cover topics that include access control, configuration management, media protection, and system and service acquisition. Ultimately, implementing these controls should result in more resilient cybersecurity defenses to ensure "ongoing federal responsibilities, critical infrastructure applications, and continuity of government".

ISA 62443

ISA 62443 is the international standard for security of industrial automation and control systems (IACS). It lists sources that the IACS Security Committee of the ISA considers exemplary of good practice. Those sources include standards, technical reports, and other related information that specify relevant implementation procedures.

CIS CSC

The CIS CSC are 20 controls specifically designed for critical infrastructure, which follow the Pareto Principle in that the first 5 controls are intended to mitigate (roughly) 85% of the risks. Those 5 controls are:

1. Inventory of authorized and unauthorized devices
2. Inventory of authorized and unauthorized software
3. Secure configurations for hardware and software
4. Continuous vulnerability assessment and remediation
5. Controlled use of administrative privileges

These 5 controls may be considered common sense. However, many organizations do not follow basic procedures like keeping inventories, tracking changes, monitoring activity, and patching known vulnerabilities.

The remaining controls are also designed to "prioritize and focus a smaller number of actions with a high pay-off, [...] derived from the most common attack patterns"[19] – thus spending a minimum amount of money for a maximum result. Most of these controls align with the protect function, though some also align to the other functions, such as the first two inventory controls listed above (identify).

How the core elements interact

To summarize, the core provides an overview of the controls your organization has in place. This core consists of four elements:

1. Functions: the five basic phases to achieve cybersecurity
2. Categories: necessary activities to fulfill each function
3. Subcategories: controls to ensure each category is addressed adequately
4. Informative references: a best-practice reference or guidance to how each subcategory can be approached

As will be demonstrated in the next chapter, the core is also used to map what your organization already does by looking at the controls already in place, and to map what you would like to do by seeing what activities would be appropriate for your organization.

Implementation – risk management

The CSF stipulates that organizations should only take cybersecurity measures that are appropriate to the risk, and "prioritize investments to maximize the impact of each dollar spent" (executive summary). Ultimately, organizations are expected to "[reduce] cybersecurity risk to critical assets and resources to levels acceptable" (Section 2.2) – a principle dating back to the origin of the Framework: President Obama's EO, which called for a **risk-based** cybersecurity framework. After

---

[19] SANS, "CIS Critical Security Controls Poster", Winter 2016, *www.cisecurity.org/wp-content/uploads/2017/03/Poster_Winter2016_CSCs.pdf*.

all, it would be foolish to invest in defenses you do not need, or to have sophisticated and expensive defenses for low-level risks.

The core also respects general risk management processes, which are:

1. Identifying risks
2. Determining level of risk in terms of impact and likelihood/frequency
3. Comparing those risks to the organization's risk appetite (risk tolerance)
4. Determining an appropriate response to the level and type of risk

Methodologies

There are several methodologies an organization can apply in assessing and managing its risks, which generally fall into two schools:

1. **Asset-based assessments**
   An asset-based risk assessment examines the threats to the organization's assets, and determines the vulnerabilities that those threats might exploit. A vulnerability without a threat cannot be exploited and, therefore, is not a risk. Equally, a threat with no vulnerability to exploit is not a risk.

2. **Scenario-based assessments**
   Scenario-based risk assessments examine the consequences of an event more generally. For instance, what harm is likely to come to the organization if there were an earthquake? What about a break-in?

Each method has benefits and drawbacks, and the organization should consider which is most appropriate to its needs.

Risk responses

Regardless of the approach taken, the organization will need to determine how to respond to risks that exceed the organization's risk appetite. In general terms, there are four types of response:

1. Avoid – terminating the source of the threat, perhaps by ending a business activity or changing the way it is done.
2. Modify – implementing security controls to reduce the impact and/or likelihood of the risk.
3. Share – transferring (part of) the risk to another party, such as through insurance.
4. Retain – actively choosing to tolerate the risk.

Naturally, retaining is only a good choice for very specific risks. There are typically four reasons for choosing to tolerate a risk:

1. The risk is within the organization's risk appetite – in other words, the risk is within a pre-defined acceptable range.
2. Mitigating the residual risk would cost too much considering its potential harm – in other words, implementing measures would be inappropriate for the level of risk.
3. It is not feasible to avoid the risk – the activity subject to the risk is essential to the organization or irreplaceable.
4. To pursue an opportunity, as some risks can have positive outcomes.

In addition, 'actual' measures – whether they consist of modifying or sharing the risk – do not have to eliminate the risk altogether, but can simply be enough to lower the risk to within acceptable boundaries. Ultimately, it is a matter of balancing the cost of treating a risk against the impact of that risk. As in many other business decisions, return on investment will remain an important principle. As the CSF points out in Section 4.0:

> Ideally, organizations using the Framework will be able to measure and assign values to their risk *along with* the cost and benefits of steps taken to reduce risk to acceptable levels. The better an organization is able to measure its risk, costs, and benefits of cybersecurity strategies and steps, the more rational, effective, and valuable its cybersecurity approach and investments will be.

In making such calculations, however, it is also important to remember that there are often legal costs and regulatory conditions behind cybersecurity. Additionally, having strong cybersecurity measures in place may well lead to new business opportunities, which in turn result in higher revenues and a bigger customer base.

To give an example of impact considerations, would the incident make the national news, local or specialist news, or simply cause a minor discussion? If it were the latter, tolerating the reputational risk may suffice, depending on the frequency of the risk and your risk appetite. If you do take actual measures, they probably would not have to be particularly major or costly. However, if the breach would be likely to make the national news, more significant and costly actions may be appropriate.

As noted above, however, there is another side to consider: some risks can be pursued for potential positive impacts, and retained on that basis. For instance, an organization may wish to move into a volatile market, which could result in significant gains or utter disaster. No matter the reason, if a decision has been made to retain a risk, this should be recorded, along with the risk owner.

Certain risk information – particularly the organization's typical cybersecurity posture and any trends – should also be passed on to stakeholders, which could include suppliers, third parties, buyers, and shareholders. For instance, it could prove useful to communicate the organization's cybersecurity risk management requirements to a potential supplier, as that supplier will need to meet those requirements too.

Ultimately, the controls that the organization ends up selecting to manage its risks will form the subcategories, which in turn will become part of the implementation plan, assuming one does not already exist.

NIST's Risk Management Framework

The core also aligns with NIST's Risk Management Framework (RMF), which is visualized in Figure 2. It provides a high-level view of a risk management cycle that draws in other NIST publications, including its CSF.

Figure 2: Visualization of the NIST Risk Management Framework[20]

The first step involves categorizing the systems within the chosen scope, and the information that is processed, stored, and transmitted by that system. This is done on the basis of an impact analysis, which is listed as a subcategory of the identify function in Appendix A of the CSF.

The second step involves the selection of a basic, initial set of security controls, which should be based on the categorization

---

[20] NIST, "Risk Management", March 2018, *https://csrc.nist.gov/projects/risk-management/risk-management-framework-(RMF)-Overview.*

in the first step. These controls will comprise the essential controls for the organization – those it is legally or contractually required to implement, and those that enable the organization to function. Then, based on a more thorough assessment of risk and local conditions, that initial set of security controls should be expanded and tailored as appropriate – much like the categories and subcategories in the Framework core.

The third step is to implement the selected controls. This should also be documented, along with the specifics of how those controls have been implemented.

The fourth step involves assessing the selected controls, ensuring that they have been implemented and are functioning correctly. Some controls will produce evidence that they are working as intended, for instance, via logs or forms filled out by workers following a defined process, while other controls will need to be actively measured or assessed.

The fifth step is where senior management comes in, and authorizes the tested and secured system. This happens on the basis of an assessment that looks at the residual risk. Management looks at the system as it operates, identifies how much risk is still present, and either authorizes it or decides that some sort of change is needed – whether it is more, fewer, or different controls.

The sixth step is to constantly monitor the authorized security controls and ensure that log collection, management, and analysis take place. This way, trends, unusual activities, and the control effectiveness can be identified and analyzed, and any changes can be documented and reported.

As the RMF is meant to be a continual cycle, you can then start again from step one, all the way through to step six to account for changes in the environment or to the system itself.

CHAPTER 3: FRAMEWORK PROFILES

The Framework profiles ('profiles') describe how cybersecurity is handled within the organization, either currently ('current profile') or as an aspiration ('target profile'). They track the organization's cybersecurity outcomes, and cybersecurity obligations and requirements, so the organization needs a solid understanding of both before it can achieve its cybersecurity objectives.

In essence, the profiles are a way for an organization to determine where its cybersecurity activities are now, and where they need to be. In other words, the profiles are an opportunity for an organization to establish a roadmap for its journey to managing cybersecurity risks more effectively. If an organization is particularly large or complex, it might develop multiple profiles, each aligned to a different component or business function.

Current profile

The current profile is a picture of an organization's current cybersecurity activities and their outcomes, and could be described as the result of a self-examination and assessment process. It is an opportunity for an organization to clearly establish its current situation with regard to its cybersecurity activities. The current profile can also be an effective way of communicating the organization's cybersecurity posture internally or with external partners.

A current profile considers the cybersecurity measures already taken – which includes any implemented controls, processes put in place, and dedicated staff. It then further considers how these existing measures align with organizational and sector goals, regulatory and contractual requirements, and industry best practices, in addition to whether they reflect established priorities.

Target profile

The target profile describes the organization's intended destination for cybersecurity risk management activities. These destinations are strongly tied to the organization's legal and regulatory requirements, contractual obligations, and business objectives.

Such objectives might be to meet minimum standards for a series of contract bids, which will probably have very clear cybersecurity objectives, or to reach a defined level of maturity, which might not have immediately apparent objectives. It could also be on the basis of trying to improve productivity because cyber attacks have caused disruptions in the past, in which case there will be metrics that the target profile can aim for.

Other factors that have presumably already influenced the current profile, and should therefore also influence the target profile, are the organization's risk appetite and resources. Some of these factors, particularly resources, may act more like constraints than guidance. As such, in some cases, the target profile may need to be adjusted to achieve organizational goals without being fanciful.

How the two profiles interact

After establishing the target profile, you can compare it to the current profile. This comparison can be used to prioritize actions necessary to achieve the intended outcomes, and to estimate the overall cost and time commitment. This can also be used as a way of measuring the progress that has already been made on the way to the target profile.

Ultimately, comparing the current and target profiles should show what still needs to be done in order to meet the organization's cybersecurity objectives. An action plan would then be developed to systematically address any gaps discovered, and prioritize them accordingly. This might be on the basis of risk, or on the basis that some are 'quick wins' whereas others have complex dependencies. The action plan could even be phased, although at that point it may be advisable to develop a number of target profiles and move forward one profile at a time.

The two profiles can also be useful for top management before and during implementation, as they can be drawn up and presented to them – which is likely a necessary step to get them to commit to the project, and view achieving the target profile as a business objective. Having clear senior management and/or board commitment to any project will also have a positive effect on the rest of the organization, reducing the chances that staff view the whole implementation process merely as a box-ticking exercise.

The most straightforward way of starting to develop the profiles is to identify how the organization relates to the Framework core. Then, the established functions, categories, and subcategories can be aligned to the organization's requirements, risk tolerance, and resources. Ultimately, the profile is simply a record of the Framework core as it applies to your organization – one outlining the current situation, and the other the intended goal.

The CSF does not provide a template for profiles, meaning that design and implementation are flexible. Some sectoral bodies have developed or proposed models for profiles, which have the added advantage that they may propose specific categories and subcategories relevant to the sector. Beyond this, the organization may wish to include additional information within its profiles, such as locations of implementation documents, the overall implementation status, board and/or management approval, and so on.

The profiles should be regularly reviewed, perhaps as part of a continual improvement cycle. These reviews can be built into the implementation process, at both the project and board level.

Target profiles may change as the organization's objectives and requirements change, whether those are related to business opportunities, legislation, or contracts, and these changes could necessitate a new action plan. Equally, target profiles may have to be adapted to new technologies or threats.

CHAPTER 4: FRAMEWORK IMPLEMENTATION TIERS

The four Framework implementation tiers ('tiers') describe different degrees of sophistication that an organization's cybersecurity measures might have – specifically on the basis of its risk management process, integrated risk management program, and external participation. The four tiers are:

1. Partial
2. Risk-informed
3. Repeatable
4. Adaptive

The tiers are designed for describing how mature an organization's risk management processes are. As the risk management processes determine how cybersecurity risks are dealt with, the tiers naturally extend to describing the rigor of the organization's cybersecurity measures. They also give an organization some idea of the characteristics of risk management at increasing levels of maturity.

How to view the tiers

That said, the organization's current tier is not immediately correlated with the success of implementation – it merely describes the state to which the implementation is achieved. For instance, if your organization has only tier one processes, implying that those processes have more than a few flaws, they can nonetheless be successful, assuming that the first tier was adequate for your organization's purposes.

As Section 2.2 of the CSF specifies, "organizations identified as Tier 1 (Partial) are encouraged to consider moving toward Tier 2 or greater". However, NIST also very clearly states that "Tiers do not represent maturity levels", although there is a clear resemblance. The CSF encourages progressing to a higher tier if it would be a cost-effective move to reducing cybersecurity risks. The 'correct' tier will enable you to meet your requirements, including business objectives and compliance obligations, without placing undue burden on the organization. However, reaching higher tiers will often mean that more business opportunities will be available to you, as you meet the criteria of more contracts.

Risk management aspects

Each tier addresses three aspects of risk management: risk management processes, the integrated risk management program, and external participation.

Risk management processes

These are the core functions of cybersecurity risk management, and range from being reactive or disconnected at the lower tiers, to a formal, consistent, and reliable set of practices at the higher tiers.

Integrated risk management program

Risk management is a crucial activity for most organizations, but it can be poorly integrated into the wider business, or across different types of risk, such as business risk, cybersecurity risk, and environmental risk. As the organization's integration of these risk programs improves, resources are more readily available, and staff across the organization gain a greater appreciation of risk management processes and cooperate more readily. Assessments and reviews also become more consistent.

External participation

Risk management is not necessarily a solely internal activity, and more mature risk management processes will seek advice and guidance from third parties, while also seeking partners and suppliers that are able to meet the organization's risk management requirements – an essential practice to limit supply chain risk. Any information from external parties will be increasingly used to update the organization's own cybersecurity measures.

A basic overview of the four tiers is provided in the following sections.

Tier 1: Partial

In the lowest tier, there are no structured or formal approaches to managing cybersecurity risks. Rather, risk is managed in an intuitive and/or reactive way – assets and the wider understanding of the organization may not have been established.

Furthermore, little to no collaboration with external parties is taking place to make sure that risk management procedures are reliable or effective, or carried out by suppliers and partners. As such, it is also generally unaware of supply chain risk.

Tier 2: Risk-informed

At the second tier, cybersecurity risk management practices are established at management level, but not organization-wide. Additionally, cybersecurity activities are prioritized based on some wider understanding of the organization, including its risk appetite and objectives.

Overall, risk management processes have been defined and implemented, key staff are aware of their roles and responsibilities, and have adequate resources available to perform them. However, other staff within the organization may or may not be aware of the cybersecurity processes because information is shared informally.

Not unlike the first tier, there is still limited collaboration with external parties, meaning that supply chains may still present a relatively high risk. Having said that, the organization is aware of its role in the larger ecosystem and the existence of risk within the supply chain.

Tier 3: Repeatable

Cybersecurity risks are now managed with consistent methods, which are documented in formal processes and policies throughout the organization. These are regularly updated based on changes in the organization's requirements or risk objectives, and changes in threats or technologies.

Staff are not just aware of their cybersecurity roles and responsibilities, and have enough resources to fulfill them – they also have adequate knowledge and skills to perform them to defined standards.

Finally, external collaboration takes place, and information is exchanged with partners. As such, supply chain risk management (SCRM) takes place. This collaboration means that risk-based management decisions can be made in response to gathered information or events that occurred to partners – potentially preventing those same events happening to your own organization, and therefore protecting your own reputation and finances.

Tier 4: Adaptive

In the highest tier, cybersecurity risk management practices are based on formal, rigorous processes, and are informed by past experiences and current activities. These contain predictive indicators, which help prevent known events from affecting your organization.

These processes are continually improved, allowing the organization to adapt its processes and policies as threats and technologies evolve, and requirements and/or risk objectives change.

Within the organization itself, there is a culture of strong cybersecurity awareness throughout, which has evolved from past experiences and information shared by external sources. Much like the third tier, staff have the knowledge, skills, and resources to perform their defined cybersecurity roles and responsibilities.

External collaboration is significantly more comprehensive and frequent, and information is actively shared with partners, allowing supply chain risks to be acted upon as quickly as possible. Ensuring that all parties are so up to date means that they can continually and proactively improve their cybersecurity systems and procedures, rather than in reaction to incidents.

How the tiers, profiles, and core interact

Ultimately, the three main points of the Framework – tiers, profiles, and core – are closely connected. If your organization decides that it wants to implement the CSF to some degree, it can determine its current profile, which in turn helps to identify its current tier. Both are informed by a variety of business needs, obligations, and objectives.

Based on its needs, the organization decides what its target profile will be. This equally informs the organization's needs for risk management and its corresponding tier. By comparing the current and target profiles, the organization develops an action plan to progress toward its target profile. A crucial element of this will be developing the necessary risk management practices.

CHAPTER 5: IMPLEMENTING THE FRAMEWORK

The CSF can be used to improve an existing cybersecurity program or to establish an entirely new one, and it offers a relatively simple implementation process that can help you go through all necessary actions for doing so. The Framework provides a seven-step process, which we expand upon and clarify below:

1. Determine objectives, priorities, and scope
2. Identify assets and risks
3. Create a current profile
4. Conduct a risk assessment
5. Create a target profile
6. Perform a gap analysis
7. Implement the action plan

Step 1: Determine objectives, priorities, and scope

First, the organization identifies its business and/or mission objectives, in addition to organizational priorities – those activities and practices without which the organization would not function. After determining objectives and priorities, you can make informed decisions about the scope of the project and the organization's risk appetite.

You will also be able to start documenting the intended plan and outline of the project, and assign key roles and responsibilities. As you are determining your scope, you should also provide a target timeframe. Giving a lot of thought to the scoping stage is critical to avoid the project dragging on or stalling, in addition to maximizing benefits.

Step 2: Identify assets and risks

Within the determined scope, you have to identify all your information assets, and any risks and/or vulnerabilities to those assets. For example, if you were to focus on your data assets only, those assets might include:

- Records of processing activities
- Customer details
- Third-party intellectual property

When considering the potential scale of the impact in the event of an incident, reputational damage can be a significant risk factor. Other possible risk factors can have personal, contractual, financial, or legal impacts – all of which could end up being costly for your organization, as they can lead to loss of revenue due to losing customers, or potentially hefty fines.

Risks that are specific to ICS, and are therefore relevant to many critical infrastructure organizations, can have impacts that include direct or indirect fatalities. Such incidents are not limited to dramatic possibilities such as factory explosions, but could also be perhaps more prosaic – but potentially just as fatal – such as power cuts or the loss of drinking water.

At this stage, you should decide on your overall risk approach, which is related to your previously determined risk appetite, but is also informed by any regulatory or contractual requirements you may have. A relatively recent possibility is New York's Cybersecurity Regulation (23 NYCRR 500).

Step 3: Create a current profile

The organization should develop a current profile, which is, as previously stated, an opportunity for an organization to clearly establish its current cybersecurity activities.

Step 4: Conduct a risk assessment

Now that the assets and their accompanying risks and/or vulnerabilities have already been identified, it is time to determine the scale of those risks and what to do about them.

Risks can be measured by combining the impact of the risk, should it materialize, with the likelihood of that risk actually occurring. This risk 'score' is often visualized in a likelihood/impact matrix, such as the one shown in Figure 3. Such a matrix is divided into different zones, in this case three, ranging from low-level or acceptable risks to high-level risks. For more guidance on how to measure cybersecurity risks, see *Information Security Risk Management for ISO27001/ISO27002.*[21]

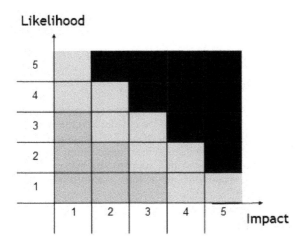

Figure 3: Example of a likelihood/impact matrix

On the basis of these risk scores, you then decide what to do with these risks. Generally speaking, there are four options – avoid, modify, share, and retain – which were discussed in the chapter on the Framework core.

---

[21] Alan Calder and Steve G Watkins, "Information Security Risk Management for ISO27001/ISO27002", April 2010, IT Governance Publishing, *www.itgovernancepublishing.co.uk/product/information-security-risk-management-for-iso27001-iso27002*.

Step 5: Create a target profile

The target profile is an opportunity to precisely define the intended outcomes of your cybersecurity project, taking everything into account that has been covered so far, which includes objectives, priorities, requirements, identified assets and risks, and stakeholder or other external input.

The CSF provides a range of categories and subcategories in Appendix A, which should be customized to meet the organization's requirements. In addition, some industry bodies have developed sector-specific profiles with relevant categories and subcategories.

Step 6: Perform a gap analysis

The gap analysis compares the current and target profiles to determine what needs to be done in order to achieve the target profile. As the CSF says in Section 3.2: "Using Profiles in this manner enables the organization to make informed decisions about cybersecurity activities, supports risk management, and enables the organization to perform cost-effective, targeted improvements."

The gap analysis will inform an action plan to address those gaps on the basis of a cost/benefit analysis and an understanding of the risks to the target profile outcomes. You should also consider what takes priority – naturally, the risks that are unacceptably high should be addressed first.

Step 7: Implement the action plan

Finally, the action plan should be executed. When implementing the agreed controls, you can refer to informative references for further guidance. The CSF lists a number of best-practice standards, guidelines, and practices, but each organization should determine for themselves which reference is the most appropriate for their sector and overall needs.

Continual improvement

These steps are intended to be repeatable, so the implemented measures are continually reviewed and improved, and the organization can progress to ever greater or more suitable levels of cybersecurity. For both the Framework and cyber resilience practices more generally, it is valuable to have continual improvement processes in place, which could mean establishing a continual improvement cycle. Ultimately, threats and technologies are far from static, so it is essential to maintain and, where necessary, improve whatever cybersecurity measures you implement.

In particular, when a breach has occurred, the practices established for the recover function should be able to both restore any assets affected and learn from the experience to improve your overall cybersecurity. However, when new requirements arise – whether these are because of a change in the industry, new regulations, or new business opportunities – the implementation model can be started again from step one – establishing a new scope – to ultimately implement a new action plan to meet your organization's new challenges.

Decision-making and implementation responsibilities

As far as the levels of decision-making and implementation are concerned, first and foremost, the executive or board deals with governance and the overall objectives and strategy, and establishes key organizational criteria, such as the risk appetite and policies.

The business or process level works within that context to develop the CSF for the organization. It defines the current and target profiles, allocates the budget, and is responsible for informing the executive level of changes in current and future risks. These changes may lead to changes in mission priorities or budget, which will have to be incorporated again into the target profile.

The implementation or operations level then actually implements the action plan derived from the current and target profiles. It also ensures the day-to-day functioning of cybersecurity controls runs smoothly. The operations level reports to the process level on implementation progress, and any changes in assets, vulnerabilities, or threats. These may, again, influence the target profile, resulting in further changes, and so on.

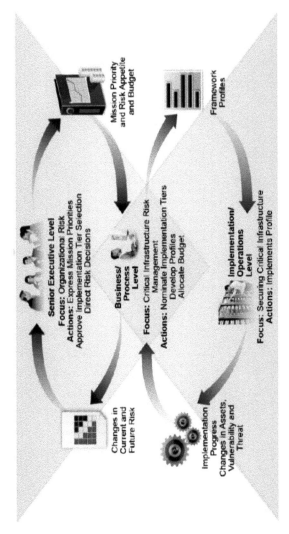

Figure 4: Typical information and decision flows within an organization (Source: Section 2.4 of the Framework)

CHAPTER 6: ALIGNMENT WITH OTHER FRAMEWORKS

Because this Framework is relatively straightforward, it would be simple to implement it as part of another implementation project, for example, becoming certified to a best-practice standard, particularly ISO 27001. It can also be implemented to help manage compliance with cybersecurity laws and regulations, such as 23 NYCRR 500, New York State's Cybersecurity Requirements for Financial Services Companies.

ISO 27001

As mentioned, ISO 27001 is an international standard, providing specifications for a best-practice ISMS. A best-practice ISMS generally focuses on protecting the organization's information assets, and as such aligns primarily with the identify, protect, and detect functions, and applies processes relevant to the respond function.

Effective cybersecurity, and therefore an effective ISMS, is founded on three 'pillars': people, processes, and technology. Ultimately, while having the right technology in place is critical to security, that technology has to be managed and maintained by people, who need to follow defined processes. This is part of the systematization of information security: ensuring full coverage at any point that information could be compromised.

ISO 27001 also has a number of principles that align with the CSF's suggestions. These include:

- Risk management
- Top management oversight
- Continual improvement

ISO 27001's risk management, much like the CSF, takes the view that risks should be treated in such a way that it "gives confidence to interested parties that risks are adequately managed" (Clause 0.1) and is "tailored to the needs of the organization" (Clause 1). In other words, any implemented measures should be cost-effective and adequate to sufficiently reduce the risk.

The Standard also mandates that top management should oversee the ISMS implementation project. Such a top-down approach ensures that the ISMS is implemented in line with the organization's overall strategic direction, and makes it clear to staff that the project is more than a mere box-ticking exercise.

A key component of an ISO 27001-compliant ISMS is penetration testing – systematic and controlled probing for vulnerabilities in your applications and networks. Many cyber attacks can easily be prevented by keeping software and systems up to date. Vulnerabilities are discovered and exploited all the time by opportunistic criminal hackers who use automated scans to identify targets. Closing these security gaps and fixing vulnerabilities as soon as they become known are essential steps to keeping your networks and information systems safe and secure.

Regular penetration testing is the most effective way of identifying exploitable vulnerabilities in your infrastructure, allowing appropriate mitigation to be applied. It is also good practice to test any new services or networks before making them available. However, regardless of whether you make use of penetration testing, your organization should continually review its ISMS to ensure that it meets the organization's needs and keeps information secure, and that changes are planned and implemented on that basis.

While the Standard mandates a continual improvement cycle, the CSF suggests subcategories "Recovery plans incorporate lessons learned" and "Recovery strategies are updated", which would only be active if an incident had actually occurred. It is important to understand the distinction between a set of ongoing processes to improve your cybersecurity and a set of controls that can only react to incidents.

ISO 22301

We have already addressed international standard ISO 22301, which provides specifications for a best-practice BCMS. Such a management system is designed to help your organization survive any disruptions, and return as quickly as possible to the status quo after such an event – in other words, designed to help make your organization as resilient as possible. As such, an ISO 22301-conformant BCMS primarily aligns to the respond and recover functions.

A BCMS aligned with ISO 22301 will reflect core practices. They include:

- Management support
- Business impact analysis (BIA)
- Risk management
- Business continuity planning

Management support has been covered earlier in this book, but it is worth reiterating that if management provides support throughout the project, staff are more likely to comply with the BCMS requirements, and indeed the overall project. As such, the overall BCMS will be more effective.

When planning to implement any management system or framework, it is important to remember that top management is unlikely to commit to a plan that has not been clearly defined. One of the first considerations should be the project's scope and objectives.

The BIA is almost certainly the most critical process involved in a BCMS. It is used to identify the organization's critical activities and their dependencies, which are in turn used to determine priorities for recovery following a disruption. The BIA will help you work out how quickly each activity needs to be resumed following an incident.

A critical outcome of the BIA is a recovery time objective (RTO) for each activity, which should also take into account that the impact of an incident usually increases with time. The RTOs will form the basis of the business continuity plan (BCP).

A BIA is not in itself enough to prepare your BCMS, however, as it only determines the value of your organization's activities. It neglects other important factors, such as:

- The specific incidents or scenarios that can affect each of these business activities
- How likely these incidents are
- How severe these incidents can be

However, a risk assessment, as previously discussed in detail, considers precisely these factors.

The content of the BCP is developed on the basis of the BIA and risk assessment, which ensures that it accurately reflects the organization's needs and specific circumstances. The BCP is the core of any BCMS. It records the actions that the organization will take in response to any incident that threatens its key activities.

BCPs often include:

- Contact details for authorities, suppliers, and other interested parties
- Calling trees featuring key staff to ensure availability of the right competence
- Checklists or steps to be taken in the case of specific events

Ultimately, the goal is to stabilize the situation, allowing the organization to continue operating despite the incident.

It is not uncommon to find organizations that do have a BCP, but not a BCMS in place. As a result, they lack the main benefits of a management system. In a full BCMS, the BCP is developed, tested, and reviewed consistently, and in line with a process that becomes more and more rigorous over time, thereby improving the BCP. In addition, employees are made aware of the existence of the BCP through a formal process, and understand their assigned roles and responsibilities in the event of an incident.

Combining ISO 27001 and ISO 22301

Even when following the CSF's guidelines, it is difficult to know whether your implementation efforts are on the right track.

We believe that the best approach to cybersecurity and resilience, and maximizing your ability to survive an attack, is to implement both an ISO 27001 ISMS and an ISO 22301 BCMS.

Both standards provide good guidance and have the advantage of already providing broad coverage of the functions outlined by the NIST Framework. Moreover, it is possible to be externally certified against both. If your organisation needs to demonstrate compliance with the CSF, accredited certification is a good way of proving cybersecurity and business continuity best practice.

They also apply a number of common processes that can be coordinated or combined to reduce the actual workload, such as training and awareness, document control, internal audits, and regular management review. These processes further support the Framework's aims by promoting good practice that benefits cybersecurity generally.

APPENDIX: KEY CHANGES FROM VERSION 1.0 TO 1.1

Update	Details
New section on self-assessment (added in retrospect; after all, the CSF is a living document, and improved with time, based on feedback and general updates)	Section 4.0, "Self-Assessing Cybersecurity Risk with the Framework", emphasizes the need for an organization to implement cost-effective measures – ultimately, the cost of treating a risk has to be balanced against the impact of that risk. And the true cost of a risk can only be estimated if the organization has examined the full picture, and taken all its needs and obligations into account. The CSF points out that an internal or third-party assessment would be a good way to understand all risk information relevant to the organization.
Expanded the CSF to make it more usable for SCRM purposes	A dedicated SCRM category (with accompanying subcategories) has been added to the Framework core. Section 3.3, "Communicating Cybersecurity Requirements with Stakeholders", has been expanded, and Section 3.4, "Buying Decisions", has been added to incorporate the SCRM focus. The stronger focus on SCRM is also reflected in the implementation tiers, where it is covered under external participation.

Clarifying the term 'compliance'	The phrase 'compliance with the Framework' is not encouraged, as it does not suit the role of the CSF.
	Following the Framework's guidance means that an organization has taken the risk-based approach required by the CSF, while 'compliance' is usually used for regulatory or contractual purposes.
	Rather than 'complying' with the Framework, the CSF is clear that it is a tool for helping organizations meet their legal, regulatory, or contractual cybersecurity requirements.

GLOSSARY

Category	Subdivisions of the Framework core's functions, organizing specific cybersecurity activities within each function.
Control	A way of managing risk, including policies, procedures, guidelines, practices, or organizational structures, which can be of an administrative, technical, management, or legal nature.
Current profile	Description of an organization's current cybersecurity activities and their outcomes.
Cyber resilience	A system of defenses *and* the ability to respond to and recover from an attack when necessary.
Event	Something that occurs (or is notable by *not* occurring) that may or may not be an incident.
Framework core	A structured description of the actual cybersecurity functions that protect an organization.
Framework profiles	Descriptions of how cybersecurity is handled within an organization, either currently or as a target.
Framework tiers	Descriptions of different degrees of sophistication that an organization's cybersecurity risk management might exhibit.

Function	Describes the primary subdivisions of cybersecurity controls within the Framework core.
Incident	An event that is likely to cause harm to the organization and/or its assets.
Informative reference	References for subcategories, specifying best-practice standards, guidelines, and practices to help achieve the intended subcategory outcomes.
ISMS	Information security management system, a systematic approach to making sure confidential or sensitive information remains secure.
Risk	Several definitions are commonly used. However, one practical definition for the purposes of this book is 'the combination of the probability of an event and its consequence'.
Risk appetite	How much risk an entity is willing to tolerate.
Risk assessment	The overall process of comparing a risk against the organization's risk appetite.
Risk management	Coordinated activities to direct and control an organization with regard to risk. Typically includes a risk assessment, risk treatment, risk acceptance, and risk communication.
Subcategory	Subdivisions of categories, describing specific results of the activities required to fulfill each category's objectives.

Target profile	Description of an organization's aspirations with regard to cybersecurity risk management activities.
Threat	A potential cause of an unwanted incident, which may result in harm to a system or organization.
Vulnerability	A weakness of an asset or group of assets that can be exploited by one or more threats.

FURTHER READING

IT Governance Publishing (ITGP) is the world's leading publisher for IT governance and compliance. Our industry-leading pocket guides, books, training resources and toolkits are written by real-world practitioners and thought leaders, and are used globally by audiences of all levels, from students to C-suite executives.

Our high-quality publications cover all IT governance, risk and compliance frameworks and are available in a range of formats. This ensures our customers can access the information they need in the way they need it.

For more information on ITGP and to view our full list of publications, please visit
www.itgovernancepublishing.co.uk.

To receive regular updates from ITGP, including information on new publications in your area(s) of interest, sign up for our newsletter   at
www.itgovernancepublishing.co.uk/topic/newsletter.

Branded publishing

Through our branded publishing service, you can customise ITGP publications with your company's branding.

Find out more at
www.itgovernancepublishing.co.uk/topic/branded-publishing-services.

Related services

ITGP is part of GRC International Group, which offers a comprehensive range of complementary products and services to help organisations meet their objectives.

For a full range of NIST resources, please visit
www.itgovernanceusa.com/shop/category/NIST-National-Institute-of-Standards-and-Technology.

Training services

The IT Governance training programme is built on our extensive practical experience designing and implementing management systems based on ISO standards, best practice and regulations.

Our courses help attendees develop practical skills and comply with contractual and regulatory requirements. They also support career development via recognised qualifications.

Learn more about our training courses and view the full course catalogue at
www.itgovernanceusa.com/training.

Professional services and consultancy

We are a leading global consultancy of IT governance, risk management and compliance solutions. We advise businesses around the world on their most critical issues and present cost-saving and risk-reducing solutions based on international best practice and frameworks.

We offer a wide range of delivery methods to suit all budgets, timescales and preferred project approaches.

Find out how our consultancy services can help your organisation at
www.itgovernanceusa.com/consulting.

Industry news

Want to stay up to date with the latest developments and resources in the IT governance and compliance market? Subscribe to our Daily Sentinel newsletter and we will send you mobile-friendly emails with fresh news and features about your preferred areas of interest, as well as unmissable offers and free resources to help you successfully start your projects:
www.itgovernanceusa.com/daily-sentinel.